Leadership

....

How to Guide Others
with Integrity

Stephen Viars

New
Growth
Press

www.newgrowthpress.com

New Growth Press, Greensboro, NC 27404
www.newgrowthpress.com
Copyright © 2012 by Stephen Viars.

Cover Design: Tandem Creative, Tom Temple,
    tandemcreative.net
Typesetting: Lisa Parnell, lparnell.com

ISBN-13: 978-1-938267-85-7
ISBN-13: 978-1-936768-41-7 (eBook)

Library of Congress Cataloging-in-Publication Data
Viars, Stephen, 1960–
  Leadership : how to guide others with integrity / Stephen Viars.
     p. cm.
  Includes bibliographical references and index.
  ISBN-13: 978-1-938267-85-7 (alk. paper)
 1. Leadership—Religious aspects—Christianity. I. Title.
  BV4597.53.L43V53   2012
  253—dc23
                                                    2012026509
Printed in Canada

20 19 18 17 16 15 14 13   2 3 4 5 6

Sally is a twenty-six-year-old reservist in the National Guard. Her commanding officer just informed her she was selected for promotion to staff sergeant. She will now be responsible for training incoming reservists from her part of the state. One part of Sally is ecstatic. She cannot wait to tell her boyfriend what has just happened. Her dad, a retired colonel in the Air Force, will be bursting with pride. Sally can practically see the broad smile on his face when he hears the news. But another side of Sally is going into overdrive as she walks down the hallway. Her heart is filling with fear and apprehension because she will be required to lead hundreds of people. She's never done that before. She wonders, *How do you lead people?*

John has just finished a ten-month deployment in the army. His wife Bonnie has done a great job leading their two young children in his absence. Out of necessity she had to be both mom and dad in many ways. Both John and Bonnie are looking forward to seeing each other again. Honestly, he can't wait to hold his wife and feel her warm embrace. In his mind he can see his children running down the hallway at the airport. When that moment comes, he is going to squeeze them until they squeal with delight. But John has heard a lot of stories from his buddies about the inevitable tension when the husband and father returns to the home.

He wants to be sure to get this right, but wonders, *How do you lead people?*

Jill just got off the phone with her pastor. Several weeks earlier the elders of her church asked her to take over the nursery ministry. There had been problems with cleanliness, organization, and morale among the people who serve, and the elders believe Jill is the perfect person to take this important ministry to the next level of excellence. Jill discussed it with her husband, and they both believe this responsibility will be a wonderful use of her organizational gifts and love for children and young families. She told her pastor yes, and he was thrilled with the news. Jill feels a sense of satisfaction because she truly believes she made a decision that honors the Lord. But now she faces a huge question: *How do you lead people?*

Frank has been on the board of the local chapter of the American Red Cross for the past six years. As a fireman, he saw firsthand how the Red Cross served families and firemen on the front lines of disaster, so he was happy to join the board when asked. But now the group has asked him to serve as board chair for the next two years. As Frank looks around the room at this group of medical professionals, business people, attorneys, and other community leaders, he finds his new position intimidating. He thinks to himself, *How do you lead people?*

How Do You Lead People in the Right Direction?

There is no cookie-cutter approach to leadership. Good leaders come in many different shapes and sizes. They grow out of a variety of backgrounds and life experiences. Sally will lead her reservist troops differently than John will lead his family. Jill's work with the nursery will not be the same as Frank's efforts with the Red Cross board. But if they are going to lead people well, they will each need to cultivate and maintain a critical component in the process—integrity. No one can lead well without integrity.

You might be surprised to hear that integrity is essential for good leadership. Perhaps you are wondering, *Why not people skills? Organizational skills? Or being an effective communicator?* It's true that you can get people to do what you want using a specific set of skills, but that is not real leadership. Real leadership is caring for and protecting those whom God has placed under your care and taking responsibility for their well-being. Godly leaders don't use their authority to take advantage of others or to make life better for themselves; instead they use their authority to help those God has given them authority over.

Sadly those in leadership often do the exact opposite—they use their authority to take advantage of those they were called to lead. All leaders are tempted to get what they want from their position of authority instead of doing what God wants and what's best for those they are leading. That's why all leaders need integrity. Without integrity you can get other people to do what you want, but you won't be doing what's best for them or what God has called you to do.

The dictionary defines *integrity* as 1) the quality or state of being complete; unbroken condition; wholeness; entirety; 2) the quality or state of being unimpaired; perfect condition; soundness; 3) the quality or state of being of sound moral principle; uprightness; honesty and sincerity. This is what Sally, John, Jill, Frank, and every other leader needs if they are going to truly care for those God has placed under their authority. Leading with integrity means others can trust that you won't lie to them or try to manipulate them. Instead you will make decisions based on what's right and what's in their best interest. The person who leads with integrity will become a complete leader—someone who doesn't just have the skills necessary for leadership, but also the character necessary to lead people well.

Of course all of us might respond by saying, "These are qualities that I don't always have. I don't feel complete and unimpaired, and I know I fall short at times when it comes to uprightness, honesty, and sincerity. Why did I accept this position when I fall so far short?"

Would you like some good news? God has given you his Word to help and guide you in becoming a leader with integrity. Paul says to Timothy (a young man who Paul was training to be a leader), "All Scripture is inspired by God and profitable for teaching, for reproof, for correction, for training in righteousness; so that the man of God may be adequate, equipped for every good work" (2 Timothy 3:16–17).

Compare the dictionary definition of integrity to what Paul explains is the purpose of the Bible. Our great Redeemer loves to glorify himself by starting with people who are weak and insufficient and making them into men and women who are adequate and equipped for every good work—people of integrity. There are many passages in God's Word to help and equip leaders, but consider the following passage:

> Therefore, having been justified by faith, we
> have peace with God through our Lord Jesus
> Christ, through whom also we have obtained
> our introduction by faith into this grace in
> which we stand; and we exult in hope of
> the glory of God. And not only this, but we
> also exult in our tribulations, knowing that
> tribulation brings about perseverance; and
> perseverance, proven character; and proven
> character, hope; and hope does not disappoint,

because the love of God has been poured out within our hearts through the Holy Spirit who was given to us. (Romans 5:1–5)

These verses give us four principles to help us lead with integrity.

Leadership Principle #1: Establish a Relationship with the Greatest Leader

In Romans 5:1, Paul describes a relationship with Jesus Christ that is real, intimate, and life-changing. In Romans, Paul explains that because of our sinful condition and inability to save ourselves, God sent his Son Jesus to die on the cross in our place. This comes to a climax in chapter 10 when Paul says, "If you confess with your mouth Jesus as Lord, and believe in your heart that God raised Him from the dead, you will be saved. . . . 'Whoever will call upon the name of the Lord will be saved'" (Romans 10:9, 13).

I hope you have this kind of relationship with Christ because knowing and relying on him is the only way you can become a leader who truly helps those under your authority. If you don't know him, now would be a great time to admit your need for Jesus and place all your faith in him. If you do know him, be assured that growing to know Jesus better is what will equip you for the leadership position God has placed you in. Whether you have been a Christian for years or have just received Christ, remember that you are not trying to become an effective leader on your own. By faith, you are personally related to the greatest leader of all time.

Jesus' character is so rich and multifaceted that many names are used in Scripture to help us understand his beauty and majesty. Several of those names emphasize what a marvelous leader Jesus is. For example, Isaiah prophesied that he would be "the mighty God" and the "Prince of Peace" (Isaiah 9:6). His disciples called him "Master" (Luke 8:24), "Teacher" (Mark 4:38), and "Lord" (Matthew 14:28). The writer of Hebrews used the picturesque "captain of their salvation" (Hebrews 2:10 NKJV) to describe the position Jesus holds in the lives of his followers.

The life of Christ is a study in leading with integrity. His words were filled with grace and power. His actions were characterized with compassion and authority. No wonder the apostle John would later summarize Jesus' life by saying, "The Word became flesh, and dwelt among us, and we saw His glory, glory as of the only begotten from the Father, full of grace and truth" (John 1:14). People from a variety of ethnic and economic conditions followed Jesus. Even after Christ ascended into heaven forty days after his resurrection, his leadership was not gone. Soon after

Jesus left this earth, the promised Holy Spirit was poured out on his followers. Jesus' promise to his disciples that he would not leave them as orphans, but would come to them became a reality (John 14:16–18). As they were filled with the Holy Spirit, they experienced the power of God to change them and equip them. The net effect was that Jesus' followers were accused of upsetting the world (Acts 17:6).

Being in relationship with Jesus means that you have the same Spirit of power, love, and self-discipline that filled him. You are in Christ (Ephesians 1:4) and he is in you (Colossians 1:27). You can humbly go to him and acknowledge your utter inability to lead others in your own strength. Imagine how powerful and effective your leadership can be as you seek to lead others in his wisdom and power. With the apostle Paul you can look over the great responsibilities God has given and proclaim "I can do all things through Him who strengthens me" (Philippians 4:13). Wise leaders never try to go at it alone, but you do not have to face this task alone if you have established a personal relationship with the greatest leader ever.

Helping Sally

What does Sally do with truth like this? She uses it to prepare herself for the challenges she faces as a leader. On the morning of her first meeting with her new team, she reminds herself as she is dressing and preparing for the day that she will not walk into the meeting room alone. As she looks in the mirror she smiles as she thinks to herself, *You are in Christ—that is what defines you and gives you direction for this day.* She takes time before she leaves the house and sits down to pray to her Lord and King, thanking him that he has promised never to leave her or forsake her. She acknowledges her fear and asks him to give strength, wisdom, and grace. She tells Jesus that she wants others to see him in the way she leads. The gospel takes away the loneliness that sometimes comes with leadership because her union with Christ through his Spirit means she is never really by herself. She is leading with integrity as she learns what it means to be complete in Christ.

Leadership Principle #2: View Yourself and Others through the Lens of God's Grace

Christ-centered leaders understand that their relationship with God is all about grace. So they view themselves and those they are leading through the lens of God's grace. Paul explained to the Ephesians "by grace you have been saved through faith; and that not of yourselves, it is the gift of God; not as a result of works, so that no one may boast" (Ephesians 2:8–9).

Paul made it clear that followers of Jesus have been introduced by faith "into this grace in which we stand"

(Romans 5:2). Your leadership potential is not simply the sum total of everything you have done in the past. Because of the marvelous gospel of Christ, you are now standing knee-deep in the grace of God. Remind yourself each day that God views you as his dearly loved child, and that he will give you daily grace for whatever troubles and challenges you will face.

Because followers of Christ now stand in the grace of God, we can rejoice that God chooses not to view us in light of our past failures, mistakes, and sins. Scripture goes so far as to say that because of God's grace, he casts our sin as far as the east is from the west (Psalm 103:12). Understanding this principle helps godly leaders respond well to the failures and shortcomings of those they are trying to lead. We should be regularly thinking things like, "because God chose to be gracious to me, I will seek to be gracious to those I have the privilege of leading today."

Grace that enables

The story of who we are in Christ continues to be amazing after we come to him in repentance and faith. Scripture teaches that the Lord chooses to relate to his children in grace. This includes the gifts and abilities that have been entrusted to us, described in God's Word as "gifts that differ according to the grace given to us" (Romans 12:6). This is what motivates Christian leaders to respond to others humbly and wisely. Whatever leadership skills we may possess are simply characteristics given to us from our generous God. This is why Paul instructed us later in Romans 12 to "be of the same mind toward one another, do not be haughty in mind, but associate with the lowly" (v. 16). We do that because we know that as we stand before others in an attempt to lead them, we are not standing in our own strength and natural abilities, but in the amazing grace of our God.

Grace that directs

Grace is free to the recipient but expensive to the giver. Basking in the free gift we received in Christ positions us to pay whatever cost is necessary to sacrificially serve others. "For you know the grace of our Lord Jesus Christ, that though He was rich, yet for your sake He became poor, so that you through His poverty might become rich" (2 Corinthians 8:9). Those we lead should know that, although they will be expected to perform at a high level of commitment and skill, those expectations will always be given in a context of grace.

Grace that sustains

Leadership can be tiring—even exhausting at times. In those times, we can turn to the gospel of Jesus Christ and find a generous supply of grace. Consider the apostle

Paul as he contemplated his terrible thorn in the flesh. Jesus' promise to him during that challenging time was, "My grace is sufficient for you, for power is perfected in weakness" (2 Corinthians 12:9). Later in the verse, Paul's response to this amazing news was, "Most gladly, therefore, I will rather boast about my weaknesses, so that the power of Christ may dwell in me."

Our position before God is not based on our inadequacies and failures. Followers of Christ stand before God clothed in the finished work of Jesus Christ. Therefore we can choose to respond to those we are called upon to lead in a way that is similar to the way he chooses to lead us. It's all about grace.

Helping John

Making a smooth transition back into the home after an extended deployment is one of the hardest challenges a soldier will face. On the one hand, John should not focus on ways he failed as a husband and father in the past. Who hasn't fallen short in all sorts of ways? The Word of God is clear: as a Christian, John stands before the threshold of his home knee-deep in God's grace.

On the other hand, John should not treat his wife and family in ways that are harsh and demanding. He can be kind and patient with his family members because he has been forever impacted by the way his heavenly Father has been kind and patient with him.

Grace helps John lead with integrity. His wholeness and completeness comes not from his own skills and abilities but from realizing his former failures have been forgiven by Christ and he now has the Spirit of Christ to help him lead his family well.

Leadership Principle #3: Seek to Glorify God

Our key passage in Romans 5 goes on to say that "we exult in the hope of the glory of God" (verse 2). Our desire is not to draw attention to ourselves but instead to live in such a way that those we lead would see Jesus in us. To glorify God is to give others the right opinion of him. People ought to have a better understanding of who God is and what he is like by observing the way we lead. Consider these crucial passages in Scripture:

> "Let your light shine before men in such
> a way that they may see your good works,
> and glorify your Father who is in heaven."
> (Matthew 5:16)

> Whether, then, you eat or drink
> or whatever you do, do all to the glory
> of God. (1 Corinthians 10:31)

Take a moment and use the following questions to consider how your leadership is helping people understand God better.

1. Do people understand more of God's mercy because of the way I respond to their mistakes?
2. Do people understand more of God's holiness because of my high ethical standards?
3. Do people understand more of God's patience because of the time I give them to grow and develop?
4. Do people understand more of God's truthfulness because of the way I communicate honestly?
5. Do people understand more of God's faithfulness because they see me keep my promises?
6. Do people understand more of God's kindness because of the tone of my voice?
7. Do people understand more of God's love because I go out of my way to help and serve them as I lead?
8. Do people understand more of God's grace because I avoid being harsh and unreasonably demanding?

If God has put you in a leadership position, why not sit down with some of those under you and ask them if they believe you glorify God in the way you lead? Question them about how your words and actions impact the way they think of God. Are they more inclined to love and serve him because of their experiences with you?

Leading like the great servant Jesus Christ

One of the many fascinating conversations Jesus had with his disciples about leadership is recorded in Matthew 20. The Lord was telling his followers about his pending death, burial, and resurrection. Regrettably his disciples were focusing on who would be greatest in Christ's kingdom. This lust for power and authority was the polar opposite of a leadership style motivated to bring glory and honor to God. They were leading selfishly for what they could get from the process. In that setting Jesus said,

> "You know that the rulers of the Gentiles lord it over them, and their great men exercise authority over them. It is not this way among you, but whoever wishes to become great among you shall be your servant, and whoever wishes to be first among you shall

be your slave; just as the Son of Man did
not come to be served, but to serve, and to
give His life a ransom for many." (Matthew
20:25–28)

There is something awe-inspiring about the pos-
sibility of functioning in a way to help others understand more fully what God is like because of their time
around us. That is why Paul said we "exult in the hope
of the glory of God" (Romans 5:2). This marvelous
goal brings clarity and purpose to the myriad of tasks
leaders face every day.

Help for Jill

Jill's willingness to lead the nursery is both a great
ministry opportunity and a potential land mine. She
will face the temptation to elevate herself and her supe-
rior organizational skills. The truth is, skills that come
naturally to her are not so easy for others. Jill may
become overly critical of the volunteers who do not
always perform to her high standards or she may even
openly condemn them for not doing things as well as
she could. In the process she will have glorified herself
and her own abilities instead of pointing others to her
Savior.

Jill needs to be sure that she focuses her energy on
the hope of glorifying God. She can still encourage

others to have high standards and a desire to serve each child and parent well. But by choosing to be a servant leader, she draws the attention not to herself, but to her Savior. The people around her will have a better picture of Jesus because they have worked under her gracious leadership. In the process, Jill is developing integrity because others see her motives for leading are genuine and sincere.

Leadership Principle #4: Embrace Leadership Challenges

Paul ends this paragraph by explaining that we can even "exult in tribulations" (Romans 5:3-5). Every person at every level of leadership knows that problems are just around the corner. But you do not have to run from the challenges—you can embrace them. Here are some reasons you don't have to fear the struggles that come with leadership.

There is potential growth in the process

Please do not make the mistake of believing that leadership is only about what God wants to do in the lives of the people you lead. There is also the issue of what the Lord is seeking to do in you. The difficulties you encounter as you lead can produce perseverance, which in turn can produce proven character.

Remember the definition of integrity you learned at the beginning of our discussion? How do you become a complete person who possesses the level of reliability, honesty, and trustworthiness that others would want to follow? The answer often comes through letting the pain of adversity draw you closer to Christ. The difficulty you are facing right now may have less to do with what God is seeking to do in the person frustrating you and more about God molding you into the image of his Son.

There is potential for great hope

The leadership challenge you are facing now might feel overwhelming. You may be tempted to quit or resort to any number of sinful ways to deal with the stress. But Paul says that as perseverance and proven character develop while we walk with Christ in the midst of the battle, we sense something else welling up in our hearts—hope. And it is not just any kind of hope, but "hope that does not disappoint" (Romans 5:5). Sometimes leaders quit just prior to the point at which God wants to take them to an entirely new level of growth and effectiveness. Those who stay faithful even when it is hard are rewarded with a new sense of hope in the power of God to help them do marvelous things.

The Holy Spirit offers power to endure

This process Paul describes is anything but a human enterprise. The verses end with the important reminder that everything we do for God is empowered "through the Holy Spirit who was given to us" (Romans 5:5). We can lead in a way that will amaze ourselves and others because of the power of the Holy Spirit working in and through us.

Sure, there will be tough spots. Sure, it will be hard. Sure, we will be tempted to be discouraged with the opposition or lack of progress. However, because it is hard does not mean it is unproductive. Embrace the leadership challenges you face with the firm expectation that the Holy Spirit can use the trial as a means of growth in your life. As you see that happen, your heart will be filled with even greater hope for the opportunities God has planned for your future.

Help for Frank

Frank's first board meeting did not go very well. One of the participants spoke disrespectfully. Someone else did not complete an assigned task. At first Frank thought about resigning. Perhaps he should just throw in the towel. But where is the integrity in that? Maybe God is trying to use this trial as a means to make Frank the complete, mature leader he wants him to be.

Instead Frank chose to continue to fulfill his role and let the process make him a more godly man. The more that process unfolds, the more Frank finds his heart filled with the kind of hope that only comes through the power of the Spirit of God. He is becoming a leader of integrity.

How about You?

In what ways has God called you to lead today? What other opportunities might be on the horizon? Why not ask him to help you become a leader of integrity?

Be sure you have a personal relationship with the greatest leader of all time and be encouraged because you will never have to lead alone. Learn to enjoy your stand in God's grace and let that become the lens through which you lead others. Pursue the goal of glorifying God and embrace the process of growth and change when the times get rough. You just might be amazed at how much God can use you. And you may be equally amazed at the way he transforms you in the process. May God help you lead with integrity.

Endnotes

1. "Integrity," *Webster's New World Dictionary* (New York: Wiley Publishing, 2003), 702.

Simple, Quick, Biblical

Advice on Complicated Counseling Issues
for Pastors, Counselors, and Individuals

MINIBOOK
CATEGORIES

- Personal Change
- Marriage & Parenting
- Medical & Psychiatric Issues

- Women's Issues
- Singles
- Military

USE YOURSELF I GIVE TO A FRIEND I DISPLAY IN YOUR CHURCH OR MINISTRY

New Growth Press

Go to **www.newgrowthpress.com** or call **336.378.7775** to purchase individual minibooks or the entire collection. Durable acrylic display stands are also available to house the minibook collection.